# Dancing with Bare Feet

Poems by

Carolyn Raphael

White Violet Press

ISBN-13: 978-0692568033

On the cover: Cantoria (choir gallery) by Luca della Robbia (circa 1400-1482), marble relief for Cathedral of Santa Maria del Fiore in Florence, detail, 1431-1438 / De Agostini Picture Library / G. Nimatallah / Bridgeman Images.

Author photo: Lawrence Raphael

*Kelsay Books*
White Violet Press
24600 Mountain Avenue 35
Hemet, California  92544

For Alfred Dorn—
poet, colleague, mentor, friend—
in remembrance

# Acknowledgments

I want to thank the editors of the publications in which the following poems, or earlier versions of them, first appeared.

*American Arts Quarterly:* "Michelangelo's Drunken *Bacchus*"
*Blue Unicorn:* "Watching," "Stalling by Woods," "Thank You for Coming"
*Edge City Review:* "Hail and Farewell"
*The Evansville Review:* "After Me"
*Iambs & Trochees:* "Scanning the Reviews"
*The Lyric:* "Between You and Me"
*Measure:* "Sprezzatura"
*Mezzo Cammin:* "My Parents' Autograph Books," "The Art of Memory"
*Nassau County Poet Laureate Society Review, 2014*: "Great-Grandma's Counsel"
*Newington-Cropsey Cultural Studies: Poetry:* "Honorable Mention"
*nycBigCityLit:* "Mnemosyne's Gift," "Very Personal Trainers"
*Oberon:* "Third-Act Blues"
*Per Contra:* "Women Who Have Lost Children"
*Pivot:* "The Next Duchess"
*Poetry Bay: Long Island Quarterly:* "Sleeping with Darth Vader"
*Poetry Digest:* "In Loco Parentis"
*Spindrifter:* "A Song of Praise," "Skin Doctor on a Nude Beach"
*String Poet:* "Swept Away"
*Theodate:* "Whistler's *Harmony in Pink and Grey: Portrait of Lady Meux*"
*Umbrella:* "Epithalamium"

These poems first appeared in *Diagrams of Bittersweet*, a chapbook published by Somers Rocks Press in 1997: "Venice in Summer," "A Word, Please."

For their generous time and invaluable advice, I thank Suzanne Noguere and Michael Palma. And for being my ever-patient sounding board, I thank my husband, Larry.

# Contents

IV.

V.

VI.

I.

# Sprezzatura

*To practise in all things a certain nonchalance which conceals all artistry and makes whatever one says or does seem uncontrived and effortless.*
         —Baldesar Castiglione, *The Book of the Courtier*, 1528
            Tr. George Bull, London, 1967

DiMaggio had it, so did Fred Astaire—
the dazzle of a sweet swing, the appealing
insouciance of a dancer on the ceiling—
the absent strain, the unassuming flair.

Since what we saw seemed natural as air,
the artistry that disallows revealing
bewitched us as we reveled in the feeling
that we could do it too, if we were there.

But elegance has shriveled into cool:
the fashion model pouting into space,
disdainful glances from the clique at school.

And accolades for apathy erase
the reverence for skill that was the rule,
while we sweep up the vestiges of grace.

# Skin Doctor on a Nude Beach

No one wants him here,
the white-coated angel of melanoma.
How foolish he looks,
in his long pants, shoes,
and hat, of course—
offering sunscreen wrapped in guilt.
He moves deliberately
from towel to blanket to chair,
asks questions in a diplomatic voice,
invading our Eden,
inviting us to know.

# Very Personal Trainers

*Venus and Adonis Health Club*

1.

A radiance of golden skin and hair,
her body firm beneath blue Lycra,
she kneels beside him,
one hand resting on his thigh.
Gently, she lifts his other leg;
their eyes look elsewhere.
Afterwards, they move to the machines:
she regulates the weights,
then counts the repetitions.
He strains, then smiles
as she whispers praise.

2.

Leaning over the table,
he presses her shoulder,
rearranges an arm.
She floods the air with banter,
cries out as he finds the ache.
Afterwards, she trudges
on the track: large step, then bend.
He walks behind her,
murmuring encouragement.
She will not turn around.

# Joe's Shoe Repair

I walked into yesterday
on mismatched vinyl squares.
Papa Geppetto, tapping a Biltrite sole,
smiled above Joe's busy hands.
Faded photos whispered
Venice, Rome, Caserta, his home town,
with a palace rivaling Versailles.
A bronze cash register
jingled its antique *fleur de lis*;
heat waves whistled from metal fins
as silver as his hair.

I saw that ceremony was required:
the greeting—brief questions briefly answered—
the diagnosis, price,
and then the pickup date,
or a finger showing where to wait.

Two wooden booths with
waist-high swinging doors,
a blue leather throne
and footstool in each one,
where a child could dream
while Mother read her paper
and waited for new heels.
Smooth wood under my fingers again,
the smell of polish,
the comfort of community.

# The Streets of Weimar

There is no litter in the streets of Weimar.
> The citizens would rise in protest, though
> there was no shout in 1937,
> when Buchenwald defaced its Beech Tree Woods.

The ovens kindled fifty thousand voices,
> just five miles north of Weimar's Theaterplatz,
> where Goethe and Schiller share the stage in bronze.

Skilled hands revived the buildings that were burned—
> the scalloped Stadthaus, trimmed in Forest Green,
> broadcasts the beauty of its renaissance.

The tourists savor dumplings, beer with bratwurst;
> and everywhere the shops sell Ginkgo plants,
> the hardy stock that pushes up through rubble.

# Kaddish for the Cardinal

*Cardinal Jean-Marie Lustiger, who was born [in Paris] to Polish Jews,*
*converted to Roman Catholicism as a boy, then rose to become*
*leader of the French church and an adviser to Pope John Paul II,*
*died Sunday . . . .*
      —John Tagliabue, *The New York Times*, August 6, 2007

Sarkozy walks past the rows of scarlet silk
to say farewell to his archbishop, born
a Jew—as I am still. How strange to see
my boyhood friend, named Aaron for his rabbi
grandfather, lie in state in Notre Dame—
to see the clergy bend to kiss his coffin.

This man, who had to wear the Star of David
sewn on his coat when Nazis raped our Paris.
Protected by a righteous Catholic,
he, then his sister, found new names for God.
I, too, found shelter in a loving house.
When Aaron was ordained as priestly Father,
*his* father witnessed from the farthest pew.
His mother's spirit called to him from Auschwitz.

It was his own request, this opening Psalm,
in French and Hebrew, read by his grand-nephew.
And then the Mourner's Kaddish, led by Arno,
the cardinal's cousin and a camp survivor.
The Aramaic rumbled down the nave.

This cardinal called himself a Christian Jew,
as did the twelve disciples. Few agreed.
But he was prized by Pope John Paul II,
who said *Amen* to prayers for harmony.
Yes, Muslims, Catholics, Jews sit here today,
but he is gone. Facing the west rose window,
the new archbishop rises from his chair.
I shiver as the Requiem Mass begins.

II.

# Sleeping with Darth Vader

*A CPAP (Continuous Positive Air Pressure) mask blows air*
*into the nose to open obstructed airways and regulate the breathing*
*during sleep of those who have Apnea.*

Those mute fermatas—I would hold my breath
until I heard you gasping back to life.
And now at night you're tethered by a hose,
air hissing softly to a background hum.
More like an ICU than marriage bed.

A little white noise insulates my sleep,
but when I wake, the harbinger returns.
Sweet Anakin, the sun declares your freedom.
It's time to breathe the balm of morning air,
to comfort me with your cheek touching mine.

# In Loco Parentis

When all was almost done with Thebes' great king,
whose pitiable fate was ironclad;
when Queen Jocasta, wild with terror, had
departed from her dreadful mothering,
the swollen-footed son still vowed to bring
the truth to light, though it might drive him mad.
This tale of marriage that the gods forbade
the stricken Chorus was compelled to sing.

But you, with greater wisdom and less pride,
refuse to seek the parents of your birth.
You turn our daughter's questioning aside
as Delphi measured truth of little worth.
Another Adam, with no God as guide,
a paradigm of self-inspired earth.

# A Word, Please

If you must sleep with my daughter
love her eyes
they're for more than flirting
they witness women bruised by fists
weep for cold men sleeping on steps
watch the gray spread in her father's hair

love her hands
they do more than fondling
they stake tall sunflowers grown from seed
smooth skittish cats toward purring ease
send notes to friends too busy to reply

love her lips
they know more than kissing
they whisper solace to a child
hold secrets that would tear a wound
crown phone calls home with lingering goodbyes

# Epithalamium

The wedding guests parade through flowery fields
with gifts and babies in their arms;
two strings, a flute sing softly in the breeze
while horses snap their tails at flies.

With gifts and babies in their arms,
the guests sit down in sun and shade;
while horses snap their tails at flies,
the slow procession moves through summer air.

The guests sit down in sun and shade
remembering, remembering . . .
The slow procession moves through summer air;
four parents weep as quiet vows are heard.

Remembering, remembering . . .
And when the magic words are said,
four parents weep as quiet vows are heard;
a newborn couple dances in the grass.

And when the magic words are said,
two strings, a flute sing softly in the breeze.
A newborn couple dances in the grass;
the wedding guests parade through flowery fields.

# A Song of Praise

*Luca della Robbia (1400?-1482) carved the Cantoria (Choir Loft) in the 1430s to decorate Florence's cathedral. Today it is installed, opposite Donatello's rival choir loft, in the Museo dell'Opera del Duomo. A picture of the panel discussed in the poem is on the cover of this book.*

*For Andrew, my first grandchild*

The last Psalm catalogues the instruments
of praise, which Luca della Robbia carved
on marble panels and placed in children's hands.
Horns, cymbals, harps, drums, strings, and tambourines.
The smallest children dance, their round limbs gleaming,
their tunics lightly draped for modesty.
I cannot help but smile or laugh out loud
to see such joy, a joy I had forgotten.

Now that you're here I feel like singing again
and dancing with bare feet, holding my ears
against the trumpet music of your cry.

# Between You and Me

Who says we have to let them fly,
these children who were bound by cords
of flesh, then need, then, finally, sky?
(I never thought I'd say these words.)

What's wrong with nesting close to home
in branches of the family tree,
where seasons, like a metronome,
count days of continuity?

Why must we always savor crumbs—
the emails, birthday cards, and calls,
the hurried holiday that numbs—
while others celebrate their smiles?

Of course we championed bravery;
who ever thought they'd fly so free?

# My Parents' Autograph Books

They lie, as do their owners, side by side.
His book is neat as shirts he always sent
out twice—to press and then perfect. Denied
a mother's smile, he knew what darkness meant.

Her book is ragged; the leather skin is flayed.
A dull gray batting bursts free from its bond
the way she gardened barefoot, disobeyed
his brown-eyed cautions with a will of blonde.

The eighth-grade entries, carved in Palmer script,
jingle their notes like a children's marching band.
*Poor ink, poor pen, poor writer, amen*, John quips;
Kay wishes Dad life *like a piano—grand.*

From 1921 and '28,
pastel forget-me-nots reverberate.

# Great-Grandma's Counsel

Dear, shut the window, draw the drapes, and swear
to shun the dampness of the cold night air.

When flying over water, say a prayer.
Bring soap and washcloths. (Do they have them there?)

No raw fish, iced drinks, burgers eaten rare;
Don't swim right after lunch; avoid sunglare.

Drive slowly, stay awake, and be aware
of teenaged drivers speeding on a dare.

The fates are always waiting, so prepare:
be sure to dress in spotless underwear.

# A Patient's Guide to Rehab after Hip Surgery

Leave your plans on the shelf; drop your pride on the floor—
your autonomous self isn't here anymore.

Call the nurse to be wheeled to the toilet or sink;
until you are healed, there is no need to think.

Every fourth day a shower in a PVC chair;
you're watered like a flower (with soap in your hair).

As you wait to be dressed; as you wait for your meals,
you've probably guessed how a four-year-old feels.

Then the therapist comes to whisk you away
for a kneebend that numbs and a stretching ballet.

Now your roommate is staring at cool Dr. Phil,
and you've given up caring about your free will.

# Archaeology

Etruscans scanned the liver to see ahead,
      their five-lobed guiding star;
I rummage through these rags for history.

On top, the remnant of my trousseau towels,
      a blue-striped signal flag,
 its edges frayed, although the fabric holds.

 One scalloped linen napkin from my mother's
      best banquet cloth. The stains
recall an undiminished family.

A terry bathrobe—larger than my husband's—
      was once my teen-aged son's.
 The child, so soon, *the father of the man*.

I note each item in my memory book
      then dig into the midden,
patiently excavating the remains.

III.

# Lie and Lay

*For my students*

A politician's life may turn awry
if he proceeds *to lay* and then *to lie.*
But your offense is far less bureaucratical,
involving only laws that are grammatical.
The verb involving falsehood you all know,
and may your conscience always tell you so.
The verb *to lie* (in this case *to lie down*)
means resting weary bones from sole to crown.
So, if your father lies down on the floor,
He's doing it in present tense, for sure.
But if his resting is a past event,
then he *lay down* is what you really meant.
*Lie* also means to *occupy a place*
(e.g., *the baseball lies near second base*).
The other verb*, to lay,* invites a snicker
from adolescents or an uptight vicar.
But it can also mean *put down*, as in,
*I lay my clothes out as a regimen.*
This present tense becomes the simple past
in, *Arthur laid his soupspoon down, at last.*
A brief review should banish all your dread—
lay down your fears; success lies straight ahead.

# The Inquisition

You realize, Mr. Chen, that you are here
because you cheated on the writing test,
the one you've failed three times. What were you thinking
of when you memorized those sentences,
the ones that we read elsewhere, word for word?

Your letter asks the committee to be fair,
but what is fair about appropriating
another person's thoughts (*appropriate*:
*to take possession of without consent—*
derived from Latin via Middle English—
and meaning, Mr. Chen, *to make one's own*)?

Your letter's moving, but it doesn't change
the facts. Besides, the syntax and the grammar
are difficult to parse.

                  Your counselor says
that you are working 30-hour weeks
plus 15 credits here. That load's too heavy.
Resolve to study more. When school is over,
there will be time for work.

                  And your speech . . . You need
to practice English, pour the sound and structure
into your ears. Speak daily with your friends;
say grace in English round the dinner table.
My boys learned French in no time flat—their prep school
instructors drove them hard; then Paris polished.

Now you may speak. . . . I'm waiting, Mr. Chen.
I cannot hear you if your face is down.
Don't mumble; speak out like a man. You're done?
Well then, the penalty will be announced
before the 24th. You'll hear from us.

# Stalling by Woods

I do not know whose woods these are.
A service station isn't far;
We crashed the pump boy's midday meal
To beg assistance for our car.

The children raised a piercing squeal
When Daddy couldn't turn the wheel,
And we all trudged through hills of snow
As cold as frozen cell phones feel.

The tow-truck man is all aglow
Because it's New Year's and we owe
The double rate—no tip, for spite.
Next year we'll fly to Mexico.

These dark woods are a tempting sight
(The children have begun to fight),
But I have poems to rewrite,
So many poems to rewrite.

# No Problem

When I say, *Thank you*, why must I hear,
*No problem*?
Who said there was a problem?
Do I care if there was?

What happened to *You're welcome*,
the gracious closing chord
that told the listener
courtesy was acknowledged?
As dead as eight-track tape decks.

I wish I could incite the old practitioners
to join in my campaign,
the ones who still write letters, make landline phone calls,
whose chivalrous response makes me feel noble—
but they are walking slowly, resting often.
They have other problems.

# Imprecations

*To the Person Who Defaced a Library Book*

May the author's name be branded on your brow,
with the title and call number, to allow
the victims of this outrage
to avenge each ruined page—
silencing all attempts to disavow.

*To the Person Who Broke Up with His Girlfriend on Facebook*

May your profile photo morph into a beast,
and your private information be released;
may you find a thousand hate notes on your wall
(with each new one the fiercest of them all),
your conversations be abruptly ended,
and you yourself increasingly unfriended.

*To the Person Who Blocked My Car*

May you need to find a bathroom
with the urgency of age.
May you boast two Broadway tickets
less than ten feet from the stage.
May your husband's special client
grow impatient at the bar—
while you hold an uncharged cell phone
and someone's blocked your car.

# The Poet Wins a Major Prize

Should a poet have a manicure?
Will it irritate my muse?
Will she stifle inspiration
if I stockpile Prada shoes?

Will Euterpe be offended
if I dye my gray hair brown?
Must I mortify my vanity
to wear the laurel crown?

Will Armani on my shoulders
and a diamond-studded phone
drive my muse to find another
and leave me on my own?

# Scanning the Reviews

I cannot praise this poet's work enough.
*Some of the poems are strong; the others, fluff.*

The suppleness of her iambic line . . . .
*Those iambs jingle like a valentine.*

Her living portraits rail, reflect, rejoice.
*Is she afraid to speak in her own voice?*

She needs to let more of her feelings show.
*She tells us much more than we need to know.*

Word-painter of Italian history—
*I ask myself, where's the epiphany?*

This is a fresh, original debut.
*I had hoped to write a positive review.*

# The Ballad of Mumbet (1744-1829)

*The grave of Elizabeth Freeman (Mumbet),*
*Sedgwick Family Plot, Stockbridge Cemetery,*
*Stockbridge, Massachusetts*

A revolution happened here,
although no blood was shed—
a former slave called Mumbet lies
among the Sedgwick dead.

As household slave in the Ashley home,
while Mumbet poured the rum,
her ears heard sounds of discontent:
rebellion's pounding drum.

She heard men speak of natural rights
in 1773,
when Ethan Allen visited
and spoke of liberty.

Soon she began to be aware
that freedom was her goal,
an inborn right that came from God,
as did her sovereign soul.

Then Mumbet took a valiant step
and saw the stakes increase.
A young white lawyer, Thomas Sedgwick,
brought suit for her release.

In August, 1781,
bold Mumbet won her suit,
then went to work in the Sedgwicks' home
to savor freedom's fruit.

She added *Freeman* to her name,
as the Ashleys had added *Mum*,
but now Bett Freeman worked with joy;
she would for years to come.

And when she died, at eighty-five,
the youngest Sedgwick penned:
*She was the most efficient helper*
*and the tenderest friend.*

She was buried in the family plot
with a stone as white as shell,
crowned by a loving testament
that read, *Good mother fare well.*

IV.

# Michelangelo's Drunken *Bacchus*

*Rome, 1497. The Florentine banker Jacopo Galli buys young*
*Michelangelo's marble statue of Bacchus from Cardinal Raffaele Riario,*
*who commissioned it but refuses to accept it on "moral" grounds.*
*Today, it can be seen in the National Museum of the Bargello in*
*Florence.*

I understand, Your Eminence. The skill
Is not in question here: the vine-wreathed head,
The wine cup, and the little satyr slyly
Purloining grapes behind the young god's feet—
Familiar echoes of the classical style.
But where is dignity—the heritage
Of Dionysus, who, said Aristotle,
Set down the cornerstone of tragic drama?
This Bacchus is a drunken youth, no more—
Reeling, with parted lips and vacant gaze.
His flesh is soft, not muscled like a god's;
The figure is androgynous and most
Unseemly for a cardinal's collection.
Have no concern, Your Eminence. Let me
Remove the Bacchus to my garden. There
My treasures gleaned from ancient Greece and Rome
May chasten him with authenticity.

# Honorable Mention

*Venice, 21 March, 1496, the dedication of Verrocchio's equestrian statue of Bartolomeo Colleoni, the mercenary. Alessandro Leopardi, who cast and finished the bronze statue after Verrocchio's death, is listening to the speeches.*

Verrocchio's statue, hah! The work is mine.
I carved my name across the horse's girth,
Designed the base with capitals and frieze
To echo buildings in the square. These hands
Adorned the helmet and the armor—*my* hands.
But who will know, and who will praise my name?
Look at the face Verrocchio left unfinished.
I drilled the pupils' fierceness in the eyes,
Raked lines of mettle on the brow, then fused
The pieces so that horse and man were one.

They say this statue is a masterpiece,
As fine as Donatello's *Gattamelata.*
Absurd! My statue puts his in the dark.
His horse's hoof rests on an orb for balance,
While my horse lifts his hoof in open air,
As if about to charge into the fray.
His condittiere sits with classic calm;
Mine stands erect, one armored shoulder raised,
Thrust forward in belligerent pursuit.
His head turns to the left, his torso, right—
A terrifying aspect of attack.

They call me to the stand for all to hear
Leopardi's name, my new post in the mint,
To see the plaque that hails a son of Venice,
Who brought to birth this noble monument.
As the cheers grow, the piazza walls resound . . . .
But history will crown Verrocchio.

# Venice in Summer

*La Fenice (The Phoenix) is Venice's famous opera house, built in 1792.
Destroyed by fire and rebuilt in 1836, it burned down again on January
29, 1996 and reopened in 2004.*

So hot that Venus floating on these waves
would bake on her own shell, yet tourists press
to view the four bronze horses (copies now)
that prance before the gold mosaic leaves
of St. Mark's splendid Byzantine excess.
Tanned gondoliers, whose whispered strokes allow
a banned endearment and illicit vow,
glide past the spot where Patriarchs once blessed
the ring that married Venice to the sea.
Rebuilt once more, Fenice scorns redress
for yet another fiery death—forgives,
content to reign in sweet-voiced harmony.
On the lagoon, with somber dignity,
the cypresses shade San Michele's graves.

# The Borghese Twins

*In 1632, Bernini finished a portrait bust of Cardinal Scipione Borghese.*
*When it was completed, the sculptor was troubled by a long fissure in the*
*marble, defacing the forehead. In fifteen nights, the story goes, he copied*
*the bust exactly. Today, both are displayed in the Villa Borghese in*
*Rome.*

Behold, Your Eminence, yourself in marble,
The way I captured you, alive. Listen
Attentively and you will hear your voice.
*(At first he smiles, but then he sees the crack*
*Across the brow—a short intake of breath.*
*The brightness in his eyes grows dull, the smile*
*Recedes. His joy falls senseless to the floor.*
*Quickly composed, he takes my arm in his;*
*Then he replies, with practiced courtesy.)*

Yes, yes, my dear Bernini, it is I,
You have me whole. Your skill is undiminished.

*(The words spell praise, but I hear disappointment:*
*A cool politeness, falling cadences.*
*One moment more, then I will end his pain . . . . )*
Your Eminence, may I commend to you
This shrouded form? Let me remove the cloth.
And so, the truer portrait of my patron.

Unkind Bernini, such a cruel jest.
Here is the prize: my perfect, speaking likeness,
With eyes that see as if they were my own.
How real the rippling of my mantle's folds,
A button half-undone as if my breath
Dislodged it. Bravo, Cavaliere, Bravo.
My portrait bust will join your coterie
In marble gathered at my villa—near,

Perhaps, Aeneas shouldering his father,
Apollo's Daphne leafing into laurel,
And David, tensed to launch the fatal stone.

# The Art of Memory

*Giordano Bruno (1548-1600), defrocked Dominican monk and radical*
*philosopher, was burned at the stake for heresy by the Roman*
*Inquisition. He was a master of memory feats.*

Before the printed word dimmed memory,
The mind was muscled to perform: to summon
Two thousand names (this said of Seneca),
Freeing the orator to dazzle crowds,
To save their song so poets could recount
Heroic tales of war and wandering.
And even after Gutenberg, the mind
Could capture words, then allocate, then hold.

Giordano Bruno, pedagogue to kings,
Performed his feats in London, Paris, Prague.
He built a memory wheel: one hundred fifty
Segments retrieved like berries from a bush.
Copernican, his books were banned, as he was,
Denied his sacraments and native soil.
At last the homesick wanderer returned—
Denounced in Venice, he was sent to Rome.
For eight hard years the Inquisition delved,
One day with questions, one with rope and wire.
The adamantine monk would not recant.

What reservoir did Bruno draw upon
To banish hunger, darkness, solitude?
Which archived images diminished time?
And in the crowded Campo dei Fiori,
Did memories console before the flames
Reached up to seal the chambers of his mind?

# The Next Duchess

*The Count's envoy reports on his visit with the Duke of Ferrara.*

My lord, I shall endeavor to relate
My meeting with Ferrara's Duke, the great
Man's elegance and courtesy, although
His lineage is foremost, as you know.
One must address the value of his name,
Its slowly burnished luster, nor can one blame
This peerless lord for guarding such a prize.
The castle's halls are endless; thus one's eyes
Are drawn to colors in the tapestries
And frescoes worked with excellence to please
The tutored palate of a connoisseur.
When the Duke paused, I needed to defer
To his request that I sit down and gaze
At his last Duchess' portrait and to praise,
I thought, the artist's skill in line and hue.
But as his silken speech spun on, I knew
His object to be otherwise. The maid
He chose was more at home with brook and glade
Than with the arduous terrain at court.
Instead of favoring her noble consort,
She beamed her sunshine equally, poor child,
On courtier or cook, and when she smiled,
Her warmth spread everywhere. This had to cease,
Lest other nobles scoff at his caprice
In choosing an unworthy bride. Commands
Were soon delivered to untitled hands
And she was gone, a sacrifice, not slaughter,
As Agamemnon parted with his daughter
For the common good. He asked me then to rise,
And as we walked downstairs, he emphasized
The depth of his regard, and, in addition,
He posed a dowry fit for his position

And your munificence. (Oh, may I add,
He owns a bronze Ravelli nymph, unclad.)
To summarize my narrative, my lord,
This is a nobleman who will afford
His Duchess wealth and privilege; meanwhile,
She merely needs to regulate her smile.

V.

# Swept Away

*The four-minute Prelude to Wagner's* Das Rheingold *is based entirely on a single chord and simulates the Rhine River.*

At first a rumble—no, an E-flat drone
Insinuates then bores into the ear.
We vibrate to the low primordial tone
That swells into a major chord. Aware
That we are riverborne, no need for air,
We yield. The undulations spread, immerse
Us deep as low bassoons and horns declare
The animation of the universe.
Then cellos, woodwinds, violins rehearse
Two leitmotifs, which we will hear retold
When Wagner weaves the fabric of the curse
An evil dwarf places on stolen gold.
The roaring current lifts us as it brings
The curtain up. The first Rhinemaiden sings.

# A Night at the Opera: *Die Walküre* at the Met

*For Larry*

Wagner remains the pinnacle for him,
especially the saga called *The Ring.*
Four operas, fifteen hours—some would trim
protracted dialogues, a wish to bring
this marathon more swiftly to a close
(a blasphemy, as any Wagnerite knows).

I must admit that now I am a fan.
It wasn't always so; there was a time
*Walküre*'s second act seemed duller than
a fifth declension Latin paradigm.
For ninety minutes nothing moved but air;
I wished I could be anywhere but there.

(Today, the English titles kindly beam
the dialogue and let the listener in.)
One night I realized a daring scheme,
an escapade I could bequeath to kin.
Before the second act I'd disappear,
returning for the third—a mutineer.

I trembled as the first-act curtain fell,
waved to my husband, ran across the street
to buy a movie ticket—I was well
into the first half hour before my feat
permitted me to watch the screen. And while
the plot was sad, I couldn't curb my smile.

After, because I had some extra time,
an ice cream soda; then I made a call
to tell my children of their mother's crime.
Claiming my vacant seat was best of all.
*Movie,* I said, and struck a victor's pose.
*Of course*, he muttered as the curtain rose.

# A Peach for Casals

*Pablo Casals refused to return to Spain as long as Franco ruled,*
*so he moved his Bach Festival to Prades, France, where he directed it*
*from 1950-1966.*

*Molitg-Les-Bains, near Prades, July, 1961*

Behind the grand hotel, I walk
through groves of palm and laurel,
twenty-year-old tourist,
a summer-perfect peach in my hand.
Cello strains draw me to a cottage—
Bach's G Major Solo Suite, the famous Prelude,
which I played as a student without promise.
Tonight I'll hear the great Casals perform
in a crowded church, where no one may applaud;
today, the maestro plays for me
as I hide beneath his open window.
Soothed by the rocking sixteenth notes, I drift until
a crescendo takes me to the crowning D,
another to the sanctuary of the final chord.
I almost applaud, almost knock but hold back.
I leave the peach on the windowsill
as an offering.

# On Deaf Ears

*As an experiment, the famous violinist Joshua Bell anonymously*
*performed several classical pieces for nearly 45 minutes in an arcade*
*outside a Washington, D.C., subway stop during morning rush hour on*
*January 12, 2007. Most people passed by without stopping, and he*
*collected a little more than $30.*
    —Based on Gene Weingarten's article "Pearls Before Breakfast"
      in *The Washington Post*, April 8, 2007

This fiddle player is a fake.
Dressed in the uniform of teens
(a long-sleeved T-shirt, cap, and jeans),
he hopes his melody will wake

up passersby who pass him by
outside a D.C. subway stop.
With open violin case as prop
he tries to catch the bleary eye

and penetrate the podded ear.
Three days before, an eager crowd
stood cheering as the maestro bowed
(they paid one hundred each to hear).

A harried mom, her son beside her,
tugs at the craning three-year-old,
who has a date with Mrs. Gold
to practice *Eensie Weensie Spider*.

The shoeshine lady fears a drop
in tips because distracting noise
has silenced coffee chat. She toys
with calling for a transit cop.

One woman knows the face, the sound,
the closed eyes, the ecstatic swaying;
one man, stopped by the brilliant playing,
stands rooted, as to sacred ground.

But most refuse to slow their pace.
Too crushed by time, too rushed for beauty,
they're caught inside the wheel of duty,
advancing as they run in place.

# Boxer at Rest

*Boxer at Rest is an anonymous Hellenic sculpture from the early 1$^{st}$
century, BCE. Found in Rome in 1885, it is bronze with copper inlay and
may be seen at the National Museum of Rome.*

Why am I drawn to this statue? I dislike boxing.
Even as a child, I left the room when
my father watched the Friday night fights on TV.
But I can't take my eyes off this man—
his battered nose and ears,
facial scars and gouges,
the blood on his arms and legs.

No idealized Greek hero, just a ruined fighter,
sitting alone after a match,
his naked body slack with weariness.
Yet how powerful his muscled arms and shoulders,
bulging calves, and lean belly.

I turn away, look back—at his expression this time.
Resignation or defeat? It's hard to tell.
The eyes are missing, but he looks over his right shoulder,
head tilted toward an unseen speaker.
His sponsor? What message?
Arms resting on his thighs, he readies himself for
the next, perhaps the final, bout.

# Whistler's *Harmony in Pink and Grey: Portrait of Lady Meux*

*Valerie Susan Langdon (1847-1910), a banjo-playing barmaid /actress, secretly married Sir Henry Meux, a wealthy London brewer and baronet.*

The soft gray background curtain sets the scene.
Downstage is Lady Meux, in afternoon dress—
Standing in profile, her face toward us—the sheen
Of cool pink satin on her train and vest.

Her gloved right hand rests primly at her side,
The same hand kissed by rich Sir Henry Meux,
Who plucked her from a dance hall. Mortified,
His family shunned her when they heard the news.

Yet Whistler rescued harmony in light
And line, transmuting fashion into art,
Wielding his brush against the social slight,
Shaping the shape that helped her play the part.

She stares defiantly, with velvet eyes,
At anyone who'd dare to criticize.

# Nefertiti's Eye

*Berlin, 1912. James Simon, a wealthy German merchant, financed the expedition that discovered the bust of Nefertiti in Amarna, Egypt. He displayed it in his home before lending and then donating it to Berlin's Egyptian Museum.*

Look at her neck, my friends, a slender stem
Of lotus. Note how the tall, blue headdress flares
Above her noble profile. Come in closer,
Where we can gaze into that storied face—
Eternal majesty, aloof, serene.
Observe the golden band that sets off arched
Black eyebrows, kohl-lined eyes. Yes, Karl, the left
Eye is unfinished. Once this troubled me.
Some say the sculptor fell in love with her
And couldn't bear to leave a perfect likeness.
I doubt the story, but I understand.
Admire her necklace, collar-wide, its rich
Design (forgive me, I have just been told
In five more minutes dinner will be served).
Say your goodbyes to Akhenaten's queen.
I, too, must bid farewell. Next week she leaves
My home to rule in the museum where all
May see those full red lips that still command.
Though I donated treasures in the past—
My bronzes, paintings . . . even my Mantegna—
She is by far the hardest to renounce.
Then I shall stand before her with the rest,
Attempting not to bend my knee in homage.
But, unlike any other, I'll recall
The days and nights I knew that she was mine.

VI.

# Do-Over

I know three women who live in their childhood houses.
One worked to make the house her own,
trying to blur the picture of her father
dying in a hospital bed in the dining room
and of her mother, scarred from the Depression,
consigning her jewelry (too good to use)
to dresser drawers.
The family ate in the basement kitchen,
saving the upstairs rooms for guests,
who hardly ever came.
When she took possession,
she scraped old memories from the floors,
painted new ones on the walls,
and sat in each room every day.

Another bought back her mother's house
and installed a new sovereign, who ruled
absolutely, as her mother had.
The walls were still spotless, and when she walked,
she raised her arms in the air
like a scrubbed surgeon,
the way she had teased her mother.
The turquoise kitchen summoned flavors
of Beef Wellington and caviar pie
eaten on Wedgwood plates with silver forks.
Her small dog yapped much like the old one
but didn't stand at the edge of the living room,
trembling. She left the telephone installed above the bathtub
but changed the plantings in the entry hall.

The third replaced her father's history books
with cookbooks, but he didn't mind—
history was built into the house.

She gave her young daughter her old bedroom,
read stories she'd been read, sang the same songs before bedtime.
Solace in the years she was a single mother.
A large mirror had always hung over the mantel
(large enough to see her daughter
descending the stairs in her prom dress,
to see herself bald from chemo treatments).
When she changed it for a smaller mirror,
she found Art Nouveau wallpaper underneath,
earlier memories than her own,
other reflections.

When I think about these women, I wonder—
how the backyard looks without the swings,
how the banister feels to a grownup hand,
how it is to make love in the parents' bedroom.
When they rewrite history,
is it better this time?
Are the old griefs counted?
Are the ghosts friendly?

# Hail and Farewell

Farewell, my golden joys of greener days,
when prodigality did not offend;
hail to the gray of winter's paraphrase.

No more the sugared apricot soufflés
or fragrant smoke from Father's custom blend.
Farewell, my golden joys of greener days.

Once-gleaming teeth have lost their snowy glaze;
now some are true while others just pretend.
Hail to the gray of winter's paraphrase.

A mirror once inspired the approving gaze
that needed no bifocals to amend.
Farewell, my golden joys of greener days.

Too loud the whispers of diminished praise
as belly, bosom, cheek, and chin descend.
Hail to the gray of winter's paraphrase.

Reluctantly I leave my fading Mays
to greet august December as a friend.
Farewell, my golden joys of greener days;
hail to the gray of winter's paraphrase.

# Third-Act Blues

I hear a preview of the closing lines,
A ghostly preview of the closing lines
That everyone recites when time assigns.

A neighbor lingers in her hospice bed,
Whispers secrets in her hospice bed
To absent lovers and the beckoning dead.

My oldest relative, who loved to talk—
This charming raconteur, who loved to talk—
Replies with words as halting as his walk.

The chemotherapy brigade is growing;
The valiant company that's always growing
Marches into forests of not knowing.

I've yet to hear *my* cues, but still I'm certain
That I'm rehearsing for the final curtain.

# Watching

She scans the face, drawn to the second hand,
as conversation whirls above her—sound
she can no longer quite decode. Enthralled,
as if the story of each numeral
were what she'd always waited for. The son
pulls down her sleeve, removing the temptation;
slowly, her eyes resume their vacant cast.
The others chatter, and the minutes pass.
With one small shift, the icon is revealed—
she gazes as the waiters serve the meal.

# Thank You for Coming

Please say your name—I have been ill;
the thunderclouds are with me still.
But now that you are here, I thrive,
a gracious gift to be alive.
I vowed to conquer, and I will.

You bring me warm regards from Bill—
I can't recall . . . . I feel a chill . . . .
Yet I'm determined to survive.
Please say your name.

Reposing in my chair, I fill
my hours with reveries until
the happy moment you arrive,
and then I manage to revive.
Who is this handing me a pill?
Please say your name.

# Mnemosyne's Gift

*Henry Gustav Molaison, 1926-2008. After an experimental brain
operation in 1953 to cure his seizures, HM developed what
neurosurgeons call "profound amnesia" and could not remember
anything for more than a few moments. This condition lasted for the rest
of his life, during which time he gave numerous interviews.*

First sunset, crunch of apple, rose perfume—
the slate erased each time. No reservoir
of angry words unchecked and peaks unclimbed.
No need to count the absent birthday cards.
And best of all, no fears about forgetting.

Visitors grieved for the diminished man,
whose memory album showed blank photographs,
who had no tale to hold a passerby.
But all who saw him noted his contentment,
his rootedness in now, eternal now.

# Women Who Have Lost Children

dress in colored mourning clothes,
choosing the patterns of despair
or camouflage in beige and gray.
The bold ones wrap themselves in scarlet
to throw a stranger off the track.

Some hide on birthdays, lighting candles
that disseminate the dark.
Some do good works and hope to thaw.
Those with appetite chew laughter,
sweet but indigestible.

The fragile ones, who never surface,
bear the day, expel the night,
and wake each morning to a funeral.

# After Me

You will survive, my rock, my smile, my balm.
An only child, you bloomed in solitude,
though now you'll wilt a while beneath a calm
gray sky that dims your classic sunny mood.
Continue reading Livy, humming Strauss
(Richard, of course), and scoring baseball games.
Please keep your passions strewn around the house,
especially the ones in picture frames.
On selfless days I want to give you leave
to find an Abishag to warm your bed
and mock the siren callings of the grave.
My wish (I like to think) for days ahead
is *Savor every sip of happiness.*
Feel free to love her well, my love, but less.

## About the Author

Carolyn Raphael retired from the English Department at Queensborough Community College, CUNY, after more than thirty years of teaching. Her poems have appeared in journals including *The Lyric, Orbis, Measure,* and *Long Island Quarterly* and on the Newington-Cropsey Cultural Studies website for the *American Arts Quarterly,* where her poem, "Honorable Mention," was nominated for a Pushcart Prize. Her chapbook, *Diagrams of Bittersweet,* was published by Somers Rocks Press in 1997, and her poetry collection, *The Most Beautiful Room in the World,* was published by David Robert Books in 2010.

Carolyn Raphael is the poetry coordinator of Great Neck Plaza in Great Neck, New York, where she ran a poetry reading series. Guests included such luminaries as X. J. Kennedy, Tom Disch, and Rhina Espaillat. Now she is working on a project called "Poetry in the Plaza," which places poems on local bulletin boards, much as "Poetry in Motion" places poems on the subway. She also coordinates the annual Great Neck Plaza Poetry Contest.

❧